Hard Hat Area

Have You Got What It Takes to Be a Contractor?

by Lisa Thompson

Compass Point Books ✥ Minneapolis, Minnesota

First American edition published in 2008 by
Compass Point Books
3109 West 50th Street, #115
Minneapolis, MN 55410

Editor: Julie Gassman
Designers: Lori Bye and James Mackey
Creative Director: Keith Griffin
Editorial Director: Nick Healy
Managing Editor: Catherine Neitge
Content Adviser: Steve Buchanan, Licensed Residential Contractor,
                Lake Mary, Florida

Editor's note: To best explain careers to readers, the author has
created composite characters based on extensive interviews and research.

This book was manufactured with paper containing
at least 10 percent post-consumer waste.
Printed in the United States of America.

Library of Congress Cataloging-in-Publication Data
Thompson, Lisa, 1969–
   Hard hat area : have you got what it takes to be a contractor? / by Lisa Thompson.
       p. cm.
   Includes index.
   ISBN 978-0-7565-3624-4 (library binding)
   1. Building trades—Vocational guidance—Juvenile literature. I. Title.
   TH159.T66 2008
   690.023—dc22   2007035556

Visit Compass Point Books on the Internet at *www.compasspointbooks.com*
or e-mail your request to *custserv@compasspointbooks.com*

Table of Contents

Hard at Work

My name is Scott, and I am a contractor. In my job, I spend my days at one building site or another. There are three things you will always find on a building site: hard work, dirt, and noise.

The building site is a hive of activity. People are hard at work with power tools—saws, drills, nail guns, and sanders. Overhead a crane maneuvers huge steel beams into place. A bobcat jerks around in the dirt. An electrician threads cables through a hole in a new wall. Plans and measurements are checked and rechecked.

This is my first site visit for the day. I ask the site manager when the roof trusses will arrive. He says there has been a mix-up with the ordering, so we are behind schedule.

I'm in the truck again, off to visit another building site. I often oversee more than one site at a time. I take a call on the road from a client wanting to know when I'll arrive for a meeting.

This is a special client with a special job. It's my young nephew, Jack. With the help of Jack and his sister, Claire, I am going to build them an incredibly awesome tree house! I tell Jack I will be there after 5 P.M.

How I Became a Contractor

Ever since I was a kid, I've liked figuring out how things could be built and building them. My uncle was a carpenter, and I worked with him on weekends and during the summer. I loved being on building sites.

In high school, I took shop class and completed small building projects ranging from a birdhouse to a coffee table.

After high school, I thought about going to a vocational school and studying to become a carpenter. But when I landed a four-year apprenticeship with a large building company, I knew it was an opportunity that I couldn't pass up.

During my apprenticeship, I got both training in the classroom and on-the-job experience. I learned about basic design, common job skills, and how to use the many tools and machines.

When the apprenticeship ended, I began working for a builder who built new houses and renovated existing ones. Six years later, I got my contractor's license. For most contracting work, a license is required. After that, I was ready to start my own business!

I think the best part about being a contractor is building something from scratch. I also love working outside and using my hands.

So, What's a Contractor?

Put simply, contractors build. A contractor organizes the workers, equipment, and materials to turn the plans for a new building into a reality. Some contractors do construction work with their own hands. Others hire and supervise subcontractors to do the work.

A contractor specializes and is licensed in one of three general types of building:
- Renovation: Fixing existing buildings
- Residential: Building new houses
- Commercial/industrial: Building commercial and industrial buildings

Clients hire the contractor to complete a project such as renovating a family home, or constructing an office building for a property developer.

Civil engineers design a commercial building to be strong enough to withstand all sorts of weather.

Architects design buildings and produce the plans the contractor will work from.

Land surveyors identify a building site's boundaries.

Contractors are always working with other people, including architects, civil engineers, hydraulic engineers, land surveyors, and suppliers. They also work with subcontractors, including specialist tradespeople, such as electricians, tilers, plumbers, and painters.

Carpenter

Tiler

Electrician

Hydraulic engineers design sewer and water-drainage systems for commercial buildings and houses.

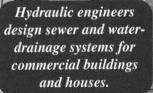

Painters

9

Carpenter and Contractor— What's the Difference?

Carpenters are skilled tradespeople who mainly work with wood. A contractor requires more training than a carpenter and leads a team of carpenters and other skilled tradespeople. The contractor is responsible for meeting with the clients and ensuring that the project is kept on schedule.

Carpenter

Contractor

Useful school subjects for becoming a contractor:

✓ math—to make quick calculations
✓ drafting—to read construction plans and be able to explain them to other people
✓ woodworking—to understand building materials and tools

To be a good contractor, you need:

✓ the ability to think in three dimensions—to visualize what something will look like when it's built
✓ strong communication skills—for working in a team
✓ good physical fitness—to endure long workdays on your feet
✓ steady balance—for working high above the ground

The Big World of Big Building

In the commercial-construction industry, contractors can work on all kinds of projects, such as office buildings, apartments, bridges, tunnels, libraries, dams, and sports stadiums.

A contractor on a commercial-construction site works with other specialized team members, like civil engineers, architects, sub-contractors, property developers, and construction crews. Often a construction manager oversees the entire project.

PUN FUN One contractor said to another, "House it going?"

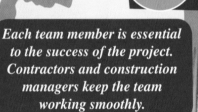

Each team member is essential to the success of the project. Contractors and construction managers keep the team working smoothly.

On an average day, a construction manager might:

- ✓ interpret plans
- ✓ estimate the quantities and costs of materials
- ✓ coordinate the supply of materials and labor
- ✓ study building contracts
- ✓ negotiate with building owners and subcontractors
- ✓ ensure that building regulations have been followed
- ✓ prepare cost estimates and documents for the next project

Can a contractor become a construction manager?

Yes! With extra training and experience on building sites, contractors can become construction managers. They coordinate the entire construction process, from initial planning through the final coat of paint.

Construction managers must have excellent attention to detail and must understand all aspects of construction. They also need to be good at managing and leading people.

Many construction managers work for large construction and development companies. Some construction managers work for government departments, while others are self-employed.

Building Basics

Structural elements

The structural elements of a building are the foundation, frame, and walls. They hold the building together. Other elements, such as roof tiles and windows, only enclose or decorate a building. Structural elements cannot be removed without damaging the strength and shape of the building.

In some designs, columns support the roof.

Load

Structures are built to withstand expected loads. The weight of a building itself is called the dead load. It doesn't move or change. The weight of objects that go in and out of a building (people, furniture, machinery, etc.) is called the live load. It moves and changes depending on what is going on in the building. A contractor must understand which materials and building techniques are appropriate for the structure's live load.

Building stresses

Gravity, wind, and other forces pushing and pulling on a building cause stresses. If the structural elements of a building are not strong enough to withstand the stresses placed on them, they will crack, twist out of shape, or even collapse.

PUN FUN

I used to be a carpenter, but then I got bored.

A building can collapse under stress.

Tension and compression

Tension and compression are the two main stresses that a building experiences. Each part of a building experiences one or the other. Compression is the result of pushing and pressing forces. Tension is the result of pulling or stretching forces.

Cracks can form in buildings under stress.

The B, C, and D of Building

A basic post and beam structure

B=Beam

A beam is a horizontal structural element that spans an opening and is supported at both ends by walls or columns. There are beams in almost every building, from small houses to huge skyscrapers. When beams and columns are the main feature of a building, it is called a "post and beam" structure.

Steel beams can span large areas.

Each floor of the Whitney Museum in New York City is cantilevered above the one below.

C=Cantilever

A cantilever is a structure that extends outward with an unsupported end. A load on the building balances the weight of the part that projects out into space. Cantilevers are common in buildings, bridges, and even the wings of airplanes. Many balconies are supported cantilevers. The balcony does not fall because it extends back into the building.

The glass and steel dome above the Reichstag building in Berlin, Germany, allows people to see the parliament in action.

Huge stone beams were lifted more than 13 feet above the ground to create Stonehenge 3,500 years ago.

D=Dome

A dome is the shape formed by a series of arches sitting on a circular base. All the surfaces of a dome are curved. Domes are very strong and are often built as roofs above round or square spaces.

PUN FUN

Good carpenters will do their work and then varnish without a trace.

Saint Basil's Cathedral in Moscow, Russia, has many domes.

BUILDING

support

Build to Last

Techniques for making strong structures

Thick beams are less likely to bend than thin beams. They also absorb vibration, making a structure stronger and more rigid.

A bridge beam, also known as a girder, needs to be very thick.

Most structures use a combination of thick and thin beams.

Cross-bracing is an excellent way to stiffen a structure. Diagonal braces squeeze together and resist lateral (sideways) forces on the structure. In commercial construction, it is often used in walls. In homes, it is sometimes used between floor beams to prevent them from twisting.

Cross-bracing adds strength to lightweight structures.

Concrete pillars, or piles, support structures built on soft soil. They are sunk deep into the earth until they rest on hard, solid soil or rock. This keeps the structure stable above ground.

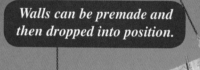

Walls can be premade and then dropped into position.

Shear walls are heavy, solid vertical walls made of reinforced concrete, brick, or stone. They give a building strength and stiffness. Shear walls resist lateral forces, such as those caused by wind and earthquakes.

Concrete will be poured around the steel reinforcing to create a shear wall, adding another story to this building.

What's It Made Of?

What you build with is just as important as how you build. Building materials have a wide variety of properties.

Brick masonry

Stone masonry

Masonry includes stone, brick, and glass blocks. Masonry handles compression well, withstanding very strong pushing and pressing forces. For this reason, it is excellent for making columns and walls. However, masonry is brittle if placed in tension and will crack if used for a long span.

Wood

Steel

Wood and steel are strong in tension, so they are often used as beams. They are also strong under compression and make strong walls and columns, just like masonry. Wood is very light relative to its strength. It is also easy to get in most parts of the world. Steel is much stronger, but it is heavy and more expensive.

Concrete is made of cement (mainly limestone and clay), gravel, sand, and water. Hardened concrete is an artificial stone, but it is as hard as natural stone after it has set. Concrete is brittle in tension, like natural stone, so it is usually poured around steel mesh or reinforcement bars (rebar), which handle the tension stresses. This is called reinforced concrete. It is used for foundations, walls, and roads.

Concrete can be pumped through pipes.

Concrete is guided into the reinforcing.

Concrete is smoothed before it sets.

Material	Pros	Cons	Uses
Brick	Cheap and strong in compression	Heavy and weak in tension	Walls, tunnels, domes
Wood	Cheap, lightweight, and moderately strong in compression and tension; a renewable resource	Rots, swells, and burns easily; can be eaten by termites	Floors and framing for walls, windows, and roofs
Steel	Strong in compression and tension; one of the strongest construction materials	Rusts; loses 90 percent of its strength in temperatures above 1,472 degrees F	Trusses, beams, and columns; cables in suspension bridges
Reinforced concrete	Strong in compression and tension; cheap, fireproof, and weatherproof; molds to any shape	Can crack as it cools and hardens; steel reinforcing can rust, cracking the concrete	Bridges, dams, foundations, domes, beams, and columns

What's in the Toolbox?

The most frequently used tools in building are the circular saw and nail gun, but there are tools for nearly every job.

Nail gun

Level

Hammer

Drill and bits

An array of nails, screws, nuts, bolts, washers, fasteners, toggles, brackets, and hinges

Adjustable wrench

Measuring tools

Carpenter's pencil

Box cutter

18.0v

Circular saw or power saw

Screwdrivers

Wait!

Hold that saw right there! Before you cut anything, remember the golden rule of building: Measure twice and cut once. Even a small mistake can waste materials and cost money.

Compound miter saw

Six Steps to Building a House

Obtain the appropriate permits before building begins. Local officials need to know that the house will meet building guidelines for the area. A city engineer reviews the building plans. Plans are often changed before they are approved and work can begin.

The land is prepared for building. A site-preparation crew clears the site of trees, rocks, and debris. If needed, they then level the site.

The formwork of a building's footings, ready for concrete

A building team marks out the area for the footings and builds the footings, base, and floor. There are various types of footings, depending on the slope of the land, the type of soil, and the type of house. A geotechnician, a type of engineer, looks at the soil and rocks on the site. Then a geotechnical report recommends what footing type to use.

Before the concrete is poured, some initial electrical and plumbing work is completed. A building inspector arrives to inspect the work. Once the inspector gives the all-clear, it's time to put up some walls.

A hardened concrete slab, ready for walls

The wall frames are either delivered ready-made—precut and even prenailed—or are made on the site. The walls are erected, followed by the trusses. Once the frame of the house is up, the building inspector returns to check the work again. When it has passed inspection, roofing contractors arrive to put on the roofing materials.

Wall framing

Roof trusses

The plumber and electrician arrive to install plumbing and electrical fittings. When the internal walls are finished, they will finish the job. The builders and carpenters fit external and internal wall linings, windows, doors, cabinets, and moldings.

The plumber and electrician finish up, and the painters take over. After a final cleanup of the site, it's time for the owners to move in!

Electricians run wiring through a building's wooden frame.

Walls are patched before being sealed and painted.

25

A Historical Perspective

King Snefru (c. 2613–2589 B.C.)

The ancient Egyptians built pyramids because they believed that life originated from mounds. So burying a king inside a pyramid meant that he would live forever. King Snefru's experiments in building pyramids influenced the building of the pyramids at Giza. His construction team moved about 126 million cubic feet of stone, and built the first true pyramid in Egypt, the Red Pyramid.

The building teams that worked on the Red Pyramid wrote their names on some of the blocks in red paint, such as the Green Gang and the Western Gang.

The Red Pyramid's 160 layers of stone took 17 years to build. Its internal burial chamber is also pyramid-shaped and supports 2 million tons of stone above it.

The Great Pyramid at Giza was built by King Snefru's son, Khufu.

Roman aqueduct

The Ancient Romans

Perhaps more than any other civilization, the Romans are famous for their amazing structures. Working with stone, bricks, concrete, and wood, they built the Colosseum in Rome and the Hagia Sophia in what is now Istanbul, Turkey. They also built aqueducts to carry water across distances as long as 59 miles.

Hagia Sophia, Istanbul

Arch of Titus, Rome

Alexandre Gustave Eiffel (1832–1923)

Eiffel was a French engineer and architect who loved math and science. He had a great understanding of how metals could be used in building—how they could be shaped and what stresses they could handle. His most famous project was the Eiffel Tower, built for the 1889 World's Fair in Paris. It was the tallest building in the world for 40 years. Eiffel also designed the internal supporting structure of the Statue of Liberty, a gift from France to the United States.

The Eiffel Tower took two years to build.

The Statue of Liberty was shipped from France to the United States in 350 pieces.

The Eiffel Tower

The curved panels of the Guggenheim Museum were cut by robot-controlled lasers.

The Guggenheim Museum, Bilbao, Spain

Frank Gehry (1929–)

Gehry is an American architect whose buildings often look like sculptures. Using the latest computer-aided design programs, Gehry designs buildings that resemble fish, ships, or crumpled pieces of paper. His most famous building is the Guggenheim Museum in Bilbao, Spain. Covered in titanium panels as thin as paper, the exterior of the museum has no flat surfaces!

Building the World's Tallest Building

Construction is under way on what will be the world's tallest building. The Burj Dubai Tower in the United Arab Emirates is due for completion in late 2008. It will reach more than 2,310 feet high. That's nearly 660 feet taller than the current tallest building, Taipei 101 in Taiwan. The shape of a desert flower influenced the design of the Burj Dubai Tower. The tower will have 160 floors built around a central core. The tower's engineers have shaped the building to minimize the effect of wind. It will contain shops, hotels, apartments, and an outdoor swimming pool on the 78th floor. The Burj Dubai Tower will feature the world's fastest elevator, rocketing skyward at nearly 40 miles per hour.

World's Other Tallest Buildings

Name: Taipei 101
Location: Taipei, Taiwan
Completed: 2004
Floors: 101
Height to spire: 1,676 feet

30

2

Name: Petronas Towers
Location: Kuala Lumpur, Malaysia
Completed: 1998
Floors: 88
Height to spire: 1,492 feet

Watch out, towers

The Shanghai World Financial Center is set to become the second tallest building in the world when the 1,614 foot tower is completed in the summer of 2008.

3

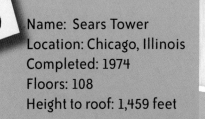

Name: Sears Tower
Location: Chicago, Illinois
Completed: 1974
Floors: 108
Height to roof: 1,459 feet

All In a Day's Work

7:30 A.M.

I get the first phone call of the day from one of my site managers. We discuss some minor changes to a job that were requested by the client.

8 A.M.

I drop off some tools to a team member working on a new house. I make sure that safety procedures are being followed, hard hats and harnesses are being worn, power tools have been certified as safe, and everyone on site knows where the closest hospital is (just in case there's an accident).

8:30 A.M.

Now I am in the office, reviewing a job quote I've been working on. Some prices for steel framing came through via e-mail yesterday, so I include them in my calculations of the cost per square foot of building area.

9:30–10:15 A.M.

I review orders for lumber needed at three building sites and call the lumberyard to make sure the frames they are making will be ready on time.

Lumberyards cut lumber to measure.

An air-powered nail gun is more efficient to use than a hammer and nail.

10:15 A.M.

The geotechnician calls. A geotechnician takes soil samples from a site before any work begins to assess the suitability of the soil for different building techniques. He also recommends the best footings for a job. We discuss a report he e-mailed me a few days ago.

10:45 A.M.

Out of the office again, this time to meet a surveyor. He has measured and marked the boundaries of a new site. Before building begins, he will mark the position of the building's footings according to the plans. There is a disagreement about a boundary line at the site. A neighbor disagrees with the surveyor's reading of the boundary.

Concrete foundations support the structure built on them.

Fortunately, it is all resolved when we sit down with the neighbor and go over the site measurements.

12:30 P.M.

I get a call from a client. She's changed her mind about the color of the tiles in her new bathroom. But I've already ordered the orange ones she wanted! Changing orders not only increases costs but also creates delays.

1 P.M.

I meet with an architect and her clients back at the office to discuss the house I am about to build for them. She has designed an environmentally friendly house that will recycle waste water to use in the garden and so reduce her clients' water bills. We discuss the latest materials and features for creating an eco-building.

2 P.M.

I make what seems like a thousand phone calls to get quotes for water tanks and pumps. I also start working on the job plan. It will show how long the house will take to build and how the job will fit into our busy schedule.

WALL CABINETS 3'-4"

BASE CABINETS & COUNTER

KITCHEN 2'-9" 3'-6"

PANTRY

W.I.C.

MASTER BEDROOM

3'-4" 6'-0"

3'-9"

FLOORING TRANSITION

DN

SHELF AND ROD

HALLWAY

OPEN TO BELOW

5'-0 1/2"

VANITY

MASTER BATHROOM

WALL CABINET

LAUNDRY

WALL CABINET

CLOSET

STAIRS

UP

9'-3"

BATHROOM
5'-10"

36 WOOD TREADS & RISERS WITH CARPET

LINE OF CONCRETE WALL

2 RISERS @ 7 3/4" MAX

3:30 P.M.

There is still time today for one last site visit. The preassembled trusses have arrived at the site (at last!), and I help the team get them up. I inspect the work, checking that it is level and square.

5:15 P.M.

I head off to meet Jack and Claire to inspect the site for their incredibly awesome tree house. I think it will take all of tomorrow to build! (I hope Jack and Claire have read the Building Basics notes I sent them a few weeks ago....)

PUN FUN When the contractor saw an air-conditioning pipe flying toward her, she duct and got out of the way.

Building the Incredibly Awesome Tree House

Site inspection
Jack and Claire show me the spot in their backyard they have chosen for the tree house. It's in the far corner of the yard, next to the big tree they are always climbing. The land is level, which is much easier to build on than sloping ground.

Plans and approval
The kids tell me their plans for the tree house. They have lots of ideas! Jack and Claire insist it must be two stories high, with a ladder connecting the levels. And they want the tree to be a part of the design.

Mom gives the OK.

Jack and Claire's tree house wish list

- ✓ veranda
- ✓ drawbridge ladder
- ✓ two levels
- ✓ viewing platforms
- ✓ slide pole
- ✓ spa pool
- ✓ tree to be part of the design
- ✓ a pulley system to lift items from ground level
- ✓ tire swing
- ✓ lots of windows
- ✓ a pizza oven

The building site

I draw up some rough plans. This gives me an idea of the tree house's size and what materials I'll need for the job. Unfortunately, not everything on Jack and Claire's wish list makes it into the plan. But we agree on a design that we are all happy with.

After Jack and Claire show the plans to their parents and get the "all clear" to build, I call the lumberyard and order the materials. I have decided to build with pine—a strong, durable and cheap wood. The lumberyard will have my order ready for pickup in the morning.

Plywood sheeting will cover the walls.

Building begins

I arrive at Jack and Claire's place early the next day with the lumber. I measure the site and mark where the tree house's supporting posts will go. I dig the holes and insert the posts. While Jack and Claire hold the posts plumb, or straight, I fill the holes with quick-set concrete.

After waiting an hour for the concrete to set, I bolt beams to the outside of the posts to form a rectangular frame around them, checking that it is level. I bolt two timber cross-members to opposite sides of the rectangle for extra stability. Then I lay the floor of the first level, always measuring twice before cutting any lumber.

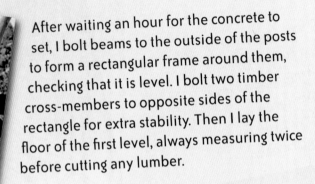

The secret of hammering

Relax your hand and arm muscles just before the hammer strikes.

The frame is finished

While Jack and Claire are making ladders, I build the second level of the tree house. Now the frame is finished— four posts and two platforms. We all agree to change our plans at this point: The first level will not have walls, but will remain just a platform.

PUN FUN   Roofers are shingle-minded.

TRAP DOOR

41

Walls, windows, and doors

I assemble some wall frames and add them to the second story. I line the walls with plywood and cut out windows from each wall. With my circular saw, I cut a trap door in the floor of the upper story for the ladder. With another saw, I cut a round hole in one corner of both levels for the sliding pole.

Wall frame ready for plywood sheeting

The roof goes on

My final frame of beams around the top of the posts will support simple roof trusses. I nail down the translucent, corrugated roofing, which will let in lots of light.

Using a circular saw is a quick way to cut plywood.

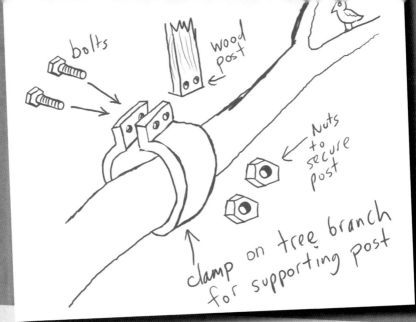

bolts

wood post

Nuts to secure post

clamp on tree branch for supporting post

Bits and pieces

I attach a ladder to the bottom story using hinges, and connect a rope swing bridge from the tree house to the tree. A few final whacks with the hammer, and we all stand back to admire the finished tree house. It has been a long day, but it was worth the effort.

"Well, what do you think?" I ask.

"It's awesome!" cry Jack and Claire in unison, as they race to the ladder.

Building is hard work, but the rewards can be addictive. No sooner is one job finished than you're planning the next one.

Claire and Jack

Opportunities for Contractors

Your skills and experience as a contractor could take you anywhere!

- Working for a construction company, ranging from a small business to a large multinational company

- Running your own construction company

- Building emergency housing in areas struck by disaster

- Specializing in certain types of construction, such as environmentally sustainable design

- Working in a related field, such as teaching, city planning, engineering, architecture, surveying, or interior design

- Serving your community by volunteering with Habitat for Humanity, a nonprofit organization that builds and renovates homes for families in need

Follow these steps to become a contractor

1. Finish school with the best grades you can get, especially in math.

2. Complete an apprenticeship in the construction industry (carpentry, electrical work, plumbing, painting, etc.). An apprenticeship combines practical, paid work with structured training to give you both experience and a certification.

3. Earn a certificate or degree from a vocational school or four-year college. Many builders first learn a trade, such as carpentry or plumbing, or a relevant skill like architectural drafting. A course on running a small business is very useful if you want to set up your own building company.

4. Even if you are not a specialized tradesperson, short courses in subjects like welding or building safety will help you supervise all the activity on a building site. Building materials and techniques are changing all the time, and you will need to keep up with the latest developments.

5. Take the required exam to earn a contractor or builder's license. Often you can take a course to prepare you for the exam.

6. Register to become a licensed contractor and consider joining an industry association, such as the Associated General Contractors of America. It offers professional recognition and opportunities for further training.

7. Being a successful contractor comes from having good working relationships with your subcontractors and suppliers, and establishing a good reputation in the industry. And remember that work on a building site starts very early. You'll probably be getting out of bed before the sun comes up!

Find Out More

- Employment opportunities for contractors are expected to increase as fast as the average overall job growth through the year 2014.
- Many employers are looking for contractors who have both construction work experience and a degree in construction management or civil engineering.
- Contractors must be available to their clients at all hours of the day. They need to be ready to deal with delays, bad weather, and job-site emergencies.
- A recent U.S. Department of Labor report showed that more than half of all contractors were self-employed.
- According to the U.S. Department of Labor, the average annual pay of construction managers (a category that includes contractors) in 2006 was $82,760. The lowest-paid 10 percent earned less than $43,200, and the highest-paid 10 percent earned more than $135,800.

Further Reading

Haslam, Andrew, and David Glover. *Building*. Princeton, N.J.: Two-Can, 2000.

Johmann, Carol A. *Skyscrapers! Super Structures to Design & Build*. Charlotte, Vt.: Williamson Publishing, 2001.

Paige, Joy. *Cool Careers Without College for People Who Love to Build Things*. New York: Rosen Publishing Group, 2002.

Parks, Peggy J. *The Sydney Opera House*. San Diego: Blackbirch Press: 2004.

On the Web

For more information on this topic, use FactHound.

1. Go to *www.facthound.com*
2. Type in this book ID: 0756536243
3. Click on the *Fetch It* button.

Glossary

apprenticeship—a work arrangement in which someone works for a skilled person, often for a basic wage, in order to learn that person's skills

architect—a person who designs buildings and advises in their construction

beam—a piece of wood, metal, or concrete used to support weight in a structure

building permit—a city-issued certificate that grants permission to carry out construction work

commercial—suitable for business use, rather than private use

compression—the stress on a structure from a force pushing or pressing against it

corrugated—having parallel rows of folds, which look like waves when seen from the edge

cross-bracing—a diagonal structural member used to strengthen a frame

dome—a rounded roof on a building

drafting—the act of producing detailed drawings

eco-building—building design that does the least possible damage to the environment

footing—the part of a foundation that touches the ground; also called footer

foundation—the lowest load-bearing part of a building

geotechnician—an engineer who investigates the soil and rock below a building site to determine the type of foundation required

lateral—relating to the sides of an object or to sideways movement

load—the amount of weight carried by a structure or part of a structure

moldings—pieces of molded wood, plaster, or plastic used for decorating a wall, door, or window

plumb line—a piece of string with a weight fixed to one end; used to test whether something is vertical

quote—an estimated cost of labor and supplies

subcontractor—a specialized tradesperson who is hired to help complete a job

span—the length between two supports, such as columns

stress—the physical pressure, pull, or other force on an object

structural elements—parts of a building that hold it together; includes the foundation, frame, and walls

tension—the stress on a structure resulting from stretching or pulling

tradespeople—people who work in a trade, such as electricians, plumbers, and carpenters

translucent—almost transparent; allowing some light to pass through

trusses—a rigid framework of beams; often form a roof

Index

Look for More Books in This Series: